Praise for William E. Krill, Jr.'s *Gentling* technique

"I read your workbook and found it very uplifting and insightful. Given my own sexual abuse history accompanied by the psychological abuse, this would have been invaluable to me during my own therapy. Every word you wrote had meaning and truth to it. As I read, I felt as though I could have been the author as you captured my thoughts, feelings, experiences and struggles, both then and now, perfectly."

—Susan Lockard

"William Krill reminds us that 'gentleness is free', but the methodology and philosophy he puts into designing a protocol for treating stress disordered children is priceless. In this book Krill directly addresses identifying stress symptoms, diagnosis and assessment tools, behavioral interpretation and a specific course of treatment to gently guide children from a place of panic, fear and defensiveness to one of a self-empowered transcendence that engages a child's natural impulse to learn. In this world where children are often disenfranchised in trauma care—and all too often treated with the same techniques as adults—Krill makes a compelling case for how to adapt proven post-trauma treatment to the world of a child."

—Michele Rosenthal, HealMyPTSD.com

"William Krill's *Gentling* is one of the most remarkable books I've ever read. The author's approach to treating PTSD in abused children employs a common sense oriented treatment that will not only help the child but will direct the clinician through the 'where do I go next?' question. This book is so needed in the world of PTSD and provides step-by-step understanding and treatment of the battered child. A must read and apply for all counselors, clinicians or anyone who is presented with the painful question, 'What can I do to help this child?'"

—Marjorie McKinnon, Author of
Repair for Kids: A Children's Program for Recovery from Incest & Childhood Sexual Abuse

"Congratulations to Krill when he says that 'being gentle' cannot be over-emphasized in work with the abused. Gentling paired with tolerance on the one hand and clear boundaries on the other will give a victim the space to begin recovery. The former emphasizes non-threatening and the latter promotes safety."

Andrew D. Gibson, PhD
Author of *Got an Angry Kid? Parenting Spike, A Seriously Difficult Child*

"William Krill's book is greatly needed. PTSD is the most common aftermath of child abuse and often domestic abuse as well. There is a critical scarcity of mental-health professionals who know how to recognize child abuse, let alone treat it. The same goes for PTSD. I am relieved that someone is filling this gaping void."

—Fr. Heyward B. Ewart, III, Ph.D.
St. James the Elder Theological Seminary

"*Gentling* breaks new ground on the subject of treating abused children. William Krill has created that rare thing: a book on an important topic that goes well beyond conventional thinking and opens up new possibilities for positive treatment outcomes. All too often in the case of abused children, the victim gets blamed for bad behavior, for withdrawing, for resisting treatment. Krill not only makes it clear that the helping professional must meet the child where he or she lives, he shows us how."

Marian Volkman, CTS, Certified TIR Trainer
Editor of *Children and Traumatic Incident Reduction*
Author of *Life Skills: Improve the Quality of Your Life*

"Krill believes that victims of child abuse have their own version of PTSD. If this child does not receive appropriate treatment, the behaviors can become worse, more embedded and harder to treat. Therefore, I believe that it is essential that people who are involved with these children especially clinicians, parents, foster parents and teachers read *Gentling*. By doing so it will help them to recognize the behaviors and deal with the child more effectively."

Paige Lovitt, *Reader Views*

"I found Krill's presentation to be very straightforward and to the point. The use of the case studies throughout the book was a wonderful way to illustrate and drive home the main points of the book. *Gentling: A Practical Guide to Treating PTSD in Abused Children* is a very thorough and comprehensive guide. I believe any mental health professional, physician, parent, or foster parent would benefit from reading this book and following the approach and techniques outlined within."

Kam Aures, *Rebecca's Reads*

The Gentling Workbook for Teen and Adult Survivors of Child Abuse

William E. Krill, Jr. L.P.C.

Loving Healing Press

Learn more at www.Gentling.org

Distributed by Ingram Book Group (USA/CAN), Bertram's Books (UK/EU)

ISBN 978-1-61599-276-8   paperback
ISBN 978-1-61599-277-5   ebook

Loving Healing Press
5145 Pontiac Trail
Ann Arbor, MI 48105

Tollfree 888-761-6268
Fax 734-663-6861
www.LHPress.com
info@LHPress.com

For Anne,
my best friend, who has dedicated her life to helping people.

Contents

Introduction

For Survivors

Recovery from the interpersonal trauma of child abuse is not an easy task, but it can be done. You will always remember, and the trauma will continue to shape your life, but it need not dominate your existence. Many teens and adults have spent years, and even decades without any treatment. This happens for a variety of reasons, including not telling anyone about the abuse, simply trying to forget the abuse and "move on," or the lack of qualified specialists to help. In some cases, the treatments that have been provided make the problem worse instead of better. Any or several of these may be part of your story.

Research shows that not everyone who has been traumatized by interpersonal abuse, or more specifically, child abuse, heals in the same way. Different people need different approaches in order to make progress in their recovery. In some cases, an individual may actually need the maturity that passing years can give in order to begin to address and treat their abuse history. One thing is certain though: *you have the power to overcome your trauma!*

While some survivors find that talking to someone about their abuse and detailing it is helpful in their recovery, others do not find this helpful. Unfortunately, there are some therapists who insist that a survivor needs to detail their abuse to another person (presumably a therapist) in order to heal. Other survivors come through their abuse with few lasting effects, and do not acquire symptoms that rise to the level of the diagnostic criteria for Post Traumatic Stress Disorder. There are some who argue that the last word, "disorder," is not always appropriate. These people find that while they have symptoms and behaviors that have developed after their abuse, they do not feel "disordered" or that their symptoms make their life so dysfunctional that they need years of specialized therapy.

There are several different approaches to treating the aftereffects of child abuse. Some people find that one of the varieties of therapy approaches available may be very effective for them. Treatments range from things like Cognitive-Behavior Therapy through Eye Movement Desensitization Reprocessing (EMDR) to specialized approaches to children like the Gentling Approach. Some survivors find great comfort and healing through spiritual practices or techniques such as mindfulness, meditation, and even physical interventions like yoga or even dancing. Since you are unique, so too will be what you need to heal from your trauma.

This workbook may be of help to you, or you may find that it is not what you need to heal, and that is OK. This workbook also may be used alongside one of the forms of healing mentioned above. This workbook could be used by an individual who is not in any formal treatment in assisting themselves in recovery, or it could be used by someone who is seeing a treatment specialist. If you decide to use the workbook, and are also getting assistance with a professional counselor or healer, it will be important for you to share the workbook with them and get their opinion about any conflicts between their work with you and the workbook approach. If you are using this workbook on your own, and it creates strong emotions and vivid memories that disrupt your current relationships or daily functioning, you are advised to seek out the help of a qualified healer before you proceed with your healing work.

You might choose to write out your answers to the questions in the workbook, or only use them to begin thinking about the particular area they speak about. Some people find writing out the answers helps them, while others do not. Remember: *you are in charge* of how you heal. The worksheets also could be used by a treatment specialist who wants to give their client some therapy homework between sessions.

Thank you for purchasing this workbook. It is my sincere hope is that it will help in some small way to move you down the path of healing and recovery.

Introduction for Clinicians:

Thank you for purchasing this workbook! I hope that it helps you in helping survivors of child abuse. After working in the mental health field as a clinician for well over thirty years, I can tell you how much I wish I'd had a clinical homework resource and protocol guide for treatment such as this when I started out.

Though the workbook was written as a collection of self-guided worksheets for a teen or adult survivor who may not have the advantage of having a clinician as a helper, it can also be used by a clinician as a means of providing between-session therapy homework, or used in an individual or group setting as a discussion starter or session focus.

The workbook language is aimed at readers with a high school reading level. If the survivors you are working with have difficulty reading, the worksheets can be read to them, used as an outline of topics for your treatment plan, or you could use only the worksheet questions with the client.

Chapter 1 – What is Abuse?

Start Your Healing Journey: Your Pace, Your Healing

Though there are similarities between people who have been abused as children, each person is unique in how they experience and heal from child abuse. The healing process takes courage, determination, and time. It is also a very private process that *you* are in control of. If you are reading this workbook, you may be at the start of your process or in the middle of it. Congratulations for starting your healing journey!

Since you are in control of your healing process, you need to decide how fast you want to move. It is suggested that you work your way through the workbook at a pace that does not cause you to have intense stress reactions. Some bad memories and bad feelings are to be expected, but these should not be so severe as to ruin your whole day or make it so you cannot take care of your responsibilities. If this happens, you might be going too fast. If you are going slowly (say one worksheet a week) and are still having severe reactions, then you should seek out a trained counselor who has experience with Post Traumatic Stress Disorder.

Remember that there are *many* paths to healing PTSD, and this workbook is only *one* of them. Not every approach or method of healing works for everyone. You owe it to yourself and your recovery to explore all the available options for healing, and become educated on each option before your decide what is right for you.

Some Questions to Think About:

How fast do you feel comfortable going through the workbook?

How will you know if you are going too fast or too slow?

Is there someone you can trust whom you can tell about your using the workbook, so that you can have some support?

Have you considered finding a counselor who specializes in treating survivors of child abuse?

The History of Child Abuse

There is probably not a time in human history when children have not been abused. Because children are small and vulnerable, they are easy victims for adults to abuse. There have been many reasons given as to why child abuse happens. There are many myths about child abuse, like it only happens in poor families or families where an adult is addicted to drugs or alcohol. But this is just not true. Child abuse occurs across all levels of income, race, cultures, and religions. The most certain thing that can be said is that there is a very good chance that adults who abuse children have been abused themselves when they were children.

Child abuse is a crime, but it has not always been so. It is only in approximately the last one hundred years that many kinds of abuse toward children have been considered to be crimes. Before our modern times, children were considered property of their parents or legal guardians. It was not illegal to deprive a child of food, water, a bed and clothes, or the ability to bathe. Any adult was able to hit a child, or even give them beatings without anyone calling the police. And child protective services as we know them are less than a hundred years old. Because sexual abuse usually remains hidden, it was one of the last kinds of abuse to get professional and legal attention.

The Child Protection movement began during the mid-1800s when the Industrial Revolution brought many people to the cities to get jobs in factories. These jobs did not pay very much, and people were extremely poor. This meant that families and children lived in conditions that were dirty, hungry, and unhealthy. The pressures of this kind of life for adults meant that many children were neglected and some were abused. Because the conditions were so bad, and some journalists began to draw attention to the slums, some good hearted people who were better off began to try and organize ways to help the poor and abused children in these situations. This effort later became known as "social work."

Since there were no laws about children having to go to school, many children worked in factory jobs for ten or twelve hours a day, six days a week. They did this to help get money to live for their families. Eventually, laws were put in place to outlaw children working some kinds of jobs, and restricted working hours. This was the beginning of society taking a hard look at how people treated children, and what laws needed to be put into place to protect children from all kinds of abuse.

Even though laws were put in place, many children were still being abused in their families. The first known time an adult was sent to jail for abusing a child was in 1874. A church social worker in New York City discovered a nine year old girl who was being neglected and beaten by her mother. At that time there were laws against animal abuse, but not child abuse. The social worker took the case to court, and argued that if animals get protection from abuse, children should too. The judge agreed, and placed the girl's mother in jail.

Thankfully, since then, more laws and services have been put in place to protect children, but children are still being abused around the world every day.

Some Questions to Think About:

In the beginning of the article it says that child abuse crosses all financial, racial, cultural, and religious backgrounds. Later in the article, it states that social work and child protection began with poor people. Why do you think child protection started that way?

Why do you think it took so long for laws to be made to protect children?

Why, even with the laws we have in place now, do you think children still get abused?

Face Up, Head Up

One of the things that can keep you from moving toward healing your history of child abuse is that you may feel ashamed of it. When a child is abused, they often begin to think that it is their fault, or that they were a bad child and deserved the abuse. Though you may have already heard this before, it is important to repeat: *no child ever deserves to be neglected, physically, emotionally, or sexually abused. I have nothing to be ashamed of!*

The feeling of shame is sometimes so strong that the survivor works very hard to try and "forget" the abuse. When you do remember it, or think about it, you might feel shame all over again. You may have gotten very good at "forgetting" the abuse by forcing yourself to only remember the good things about your family, or the abuser. You may also work hard at minimizing the abuse. Another aspect of shame is that sooner or later, a child realizes that not every adult treats children the way that they were treated. You may have developed a feeling of shame around the fact that someone close to you treated you that way, and you don't want others to find out.

But no one who was abused as child really forgets what happened. You may not remember all of the details, or the order of the events very clearly, but you do not forget the abuse and pain it had caused. If you choose to talk to someone about the details of your abuse, or even if you decide to keep those details private, it is important that you move toward facing the abuse trauma you have experienced. And what does "facing" the abuse episode(s) mean?

It means that you stop wasting your energy on trying to push the abuse from your mind in an attempt to control the bad feelings bad memories give you. Instead of *pretending* that everything is OK and nothing ever happened, you let yourself go through the emotions and find new ways to be *really* OK.

Many survivors find it helpful to spend time thinking about their abuse issues and *processing* them. Processing means that you take an objective look at the abuse. This is by no means easy, because it can create intense feelings. Remember that you survived the actual abuse, so you can also survive looking at it in detail if you choose to do so. When you look at your abuse in detail, especially if you do this with someone you trust and who believes in you, you can get a better perspective about what happened and exactly *who is responsible* for the abuse.

When you work at moving from being a victim to a survivor of abuse, you can be proud of yourself for taking responsibility for your own healing. You can be proud that you are keeping yourself from continuing to be hurt and damaged from the abuse you survived. You can be proud that you are no longer letting the person or people who abused you to control your life and your happiness.

You can hold your head up.

Some Questions to Think About:

Do you feel shame over the abuse that you have survived?

What *part* of the abuse causes you the most feelings of shame?

Have you tried to 'forget' the abuse? Did it work?

How do you feel about processing your abuse by talking about the details to someone?

Have you ever thought to feel proud that you *survived* child abuse?

Types of Abuse

Child abuse is most often classified into four different categories: neglect, emotional abuse, physical abuse, and sexual abuse. These categories are ways of describing abuse types and abuse behaviors of adults toward children. Each of them will be described below.

It is important to understand that the four categories overlap. Whenever a child is abused, the child will suffer strong emotions. Neglect, physical abuse, and sexual abuse are always emotionally abusive to a child, but emotional abuse can exist on its own without the other three being present. Sexual abuse is definitely physical abuse, but not all physical abuse is sexual.

It is also important to understand that there is a difference between legal definitions of child abuse and what many people feel is abusive. "Neglect," for example, might mean for some people that a child does not have a new coat for the beginning of a school year, when legally, if the child has an old, used, but warm coat for winter, there is no neglect. Another example is physical abuse. Some people feel that spanking a child is abuse, but in most places, it is not legally abuse. Only if the child has visible physical damage, or medically confirmed internal damage is physical abuse considered.

While there are many definitions of abuse, we will use the following for discussion:

Neglect: When a child in the care of an adult is not given enough food, shelter, clothing that is proper for the season, or is not getting the child medical help or medicine when it is needed. Neglect also includes insufficient supervision to guard the child against danger.

Emotional Abuse: When a child in the care of an adult is consistently teased, harassed, punished in humiliating ways, exposed to adult violence, terrorized with threats or other frightening stories or images, constantly manipulated, or given habitual false promises.

Physical Abuse: Any physical contact with a child by an adult that produces physical damage, pain, or has a life-long effect on the child's physical or intellectual functioning.

Sexual Abuse: Any physical, verbal, or written contact between an adult and child that is sexual in nature. Any intentional or repeated accidental exposure of a child to sexual interaction between adults or exposure to materials that are of an adult sexual nature is abuse. This definition excludes: helping a child to bathe or dress, needed medical attention, or legitimate sexual education.

Some Questions to Think About:

The article says that there is a difference between what people think is abuse, and what the law says is abuse. Should child abuse laws be stronger and more clearly defined?

The different types of child abuse often overlap. Do you think that there are situations where three or even four types overlap?

Are there any missing characteristics in the definitions of child abuse above that you think should be Included?

Neglect

Directions: Below are some questions about child neglect. You are invited to jot down some notes about each question to discuss with your counselor later. While many people find writing things down about their abuse helps, other people are uncomfortable doing so. If writing down details about your abuse is too painful, just give each question some private thought.

How often do you think about or suddenly remember things about your neglect as a child?

What feelings do you have when you remember?

Is there any one situation or episode of neglect that stands out in your memory?

Are you able to write it down or describe it?

How old were you when you were neglected?

Did you feel like you were being neglected when you were a child?

How did being neglected affect your friendships and school life?

If you were abused in more than one way, do you have different feelings about the different ways?

Emotional Abuse

Directions: Below are some questions about child emotional abuse. You are invited to jot down some notes about each question to discuss with your counselor later. While many people find writing things down about their abuse helps, other people are uncomfortable doing so. If writing down details about your abuse is too painful, just give each question some private thought.

How often do you think about or suddenly remember things about your emotional abuse as a child?

What feelings do you have when you remember?

Is there any one situation or episode of emotional abuse that stands out in your memory?

Are you able to write it down or describe it?

How old were you when you were emotionally abused?

Did you feel like you were being abused at the time, when you were a child?

If so, how did that affect your friendships and school life?

If you were abused in more than one way, do you have different feelings about the different ways?

Physical Abuse

Directions: Below are some questions about child physical abuse. You are invited to jot down some notes about each question to discuss with your counselor later. While many people find writing things down about their abuse helps, other people are uncomfortable doing so. If writing down details about your abuse is too painful, just give each question some private thought.

How often do you think about or suddenly remember things about your physical abuse as a child?

What feelings do you have when you remember?

Is there any one situation or episode of physical abuse that stands out in your memory?

Are you able to write it down or describe it?

How old were you when you were physically abused?

Did you feel like you were being abused when you were a child?

If so, how did that affect your friendships and school life?

If you were abused in more than one way, do you have different feelings about the different ways?

Sexual Abuse

Directions: Below are some questions about child sexual abuse. You are invited to jot down some notes about each question to discuss with your counselor later. While many people find writing things down about their abuse helps, other people are uncomfortable doing so. If writing down details about your abuse is too painful, just give each question some private thought.

How often do you think about or suddenly remember things about your sexual abuse as a child?

What feelings do you have when you remember?

Is there any one situation or episode of sexual abuse that stands out in your memory?

Are you able to write it down or describe it?

How old were you when you were sexually abused?

Did you feel like you were being abused when you were a child?

If so, how did that affect your friendships and school life?

If you were abused in more than one way, do you have different feelings about the different ways?

Different Kinds of Sexual Abuse

Not all childhood sexual abuse is the same. Some people were abused by a stranger, while more often, the perpetrator was someone known to the child or family, like a neighbor, or friend of a parent. Still more often, a child may have been sexually abused by an immediate family member (like parent or sibling, or grandparent).

When a child is sexually abused, the *way* that the abuser gets the child to do sexual things can vary. One abuser may threaten, frighten, or force the child into doing sexual things. Since the adult is bigger and stronger, the child does what the adult tells them to do. Another kind of abuser may try to do nice things for a child, like give gifts or special food to get the child to cooperate with the sexual behaviors. Other abusers may enforce cooperation by threatening to hurt the child's pet or another family member. Still other abusers might say nothing to the child, but just start doing sexual things around the child or to the child. Abusers may accuse the child of appearing 'too sexy' and somehow inviting the abuser to make sexual advances on the child.

What sexual things the abuser does can also be different for different survivors of sexual abuse. Some abusers may expose the child to sexual images (like movies or pictures), or expose the child to seeing the abuser nude or masturbating. Still others may force a child to watch adults having sex, or force the child to do something sexual to another child. Other abusers may touch the child in sexual ways, or force the child to touch the abuser in sexual ways. This usually includes touching genitals (private parts). Other sexual abuse activities may include oral sex and penetration of the child's vagina or anus with the abuser's fingers or (if the abuser is a male) their penis. Sometimes objects are used to do this.

Many children experience sexual abuse as frightening or disgusting, but some children do find the sexual abuse to feel good, at least at first. It is especially difficult when the child experiences physical pleasure during the sexual abuse, because when they find out that it is wrong, they may feel very guilty about the good feelings that the sexual abuse produced at the time.

Because everyone enjoys touch, and sexual behaviors feel good, these things may feel good to a child. It is not the physical pleasure of touch or sexual behaviors that are "bad," *but it is the fact that the adult is doing this with a child that is bad*. Because the child is human, their body may respond with feelings of pleasure. And no one should feel shame about that.

It is important to remember that ALL of the ways the abuser gets the child to do sexual things and ALL of these behaviors that an abuser may do to a child are all sexual abuse. All of them are hurtful to a child's emotions, body, and spirit. All of these things can have negative effects in the child's life as they grow into their teen and adult years. Each of these behaviors are damaging, and none of them are "worse" or "less bad" than the others.

Some Questions to Think About:

What approach did your abuser use?

Are you able to speak about the details of your sexual abuse?

If you are not able to speak about the details, are you able to write them down?

Was your abuse frightening to you, make you feel angry, or disgust you at the time of the abuse?

Chapter 2 – Symptoms of Abuse

Confusing Emotions

When a child is neglected, physically abused, or sexually abused by someone they know, especially a family member, they will have very confused emotions about the abuser and about themselves.

Every child naturally looks to their parents and family members to be people that they can trust and who care for them and love them. When a family member is abusive, the child gets a very "mixed message" about this person. On the one hand, the child loves, cares for, and wants to trust the family member. On the other hand, the child may feel a great deal of anger, mistrust, and rage at this person because of the abuse.

Such strong feelings that do not match are confusing to the child, and very difficult to figure out and come to terms with. The child will often begin to feel responsible for the way the adult is treating them, and therefore will begin to try very hard to be "extra good" so that the adult abuser will not repeat the abusive behavior. The child becomes further confused when this does not seem to work.

A child who is abused by a family member often begins to feel very, very angry at the abuser while at the same time having feelings of love for this person. For example, a child may be very angry at their parent who often gets drunk or high, and cannot take care of the child properly. But the child may have strong feelings of worry and wanting to take care of the parent when the parent is intoxicated or recovering from being intoxicated.

In cases of sexual abuse, the child may have been told by the adult that the sex is a demonstration of love and a sign of affection. But sooner or later, the child begins to feel that something is very wrong, because after the sexual contact, the child does not feel good or loved. They just feel bad.

Some children who have been sexually abused may have experienced sensations of physical pleasure from the sexual contact. This can be very confusing to a child's emotions and thinking. While the sexual contact felt good, they are left with emotions that make them feel quite uncomfortable, sad, angry, or dirty. They may also later feel very guilty and ashamed about the sexual contact when they discover that it is really abuse and it is breaking a law.

Some Questions to Think About:

Did you have confusing emotions when you were a child?

Can you name the feelings that you had, both the negative ones and the positive ones?

Did you blame yourself for your abuse?

How did you manage your negative emotions about your abuse when you were a child?

The Perpetrator

Directions: Below are a few statements and then some questions about perpetrators. You are invited to jot down some notes about each question to discuss with your counselor later. While many people find that writing things down about their perpetrator helps, other people are uncomfortable doing so. If writing down details about your perpetrator is too painful, just give each question some private thought.

"Perpetrator" is a law enforcement and legal word used to describe a person who commits a crime. The perpetrator of child abuse is quite often someone the child knows and trusts. It can be a parent, sibling, or a grandparent or other relative. It can be a step-parent. Less frequently, it is a teacher, counselor, coach, or religious leader. Less frequently still, it is a stranger.

Most abuse survivors have very complex and strong feelings about their perpetrator. Some people have more than one perpetrator. These complex feelings are normal, and you should not feel badly about this. This worksheet is designed to help you work through those feelings.

Who was your perpetrator?

If your perpetrator was close to you, do you remember anything good about them or your relationship with them?

What physical characteristics stand out to you about your perpetrator?

Did your perpetrator abuse alcohol or drugs?

Do you know if your perpetrator abused other children?

Do you think other adults knew about your abuse and who was doing it?

Did you ever try and tell someone or get help to stop the abuse?

If your answer is 'no' to the above question, do you feel guilty about not telling or getting help?

If you feel comfortable enough, could you write down or talk about a detailed account of an episode of abuse?

Describe ALL of the feelings that you have about your perpetrator.

How long did your abuse last?

Why Abuse Is Wrong

Asking why abuse is so wrong might sound a bit strange. Most everyone *knows* that abuse of a child is wrong, but understanding *why* it is wrong is important for the survivor of abuse to understand. Many abused children are 'brainwashed' by their abuser into thinking that the abuse is somehow their own fault. They are told that because the child did something "bad," this somehow forced the adult abuser to do the abuse. Or, the abuser tells the child that what is going on is not bad in any way. These are of course, all lies.

Abuse by one person of another is always wrong because it involves an imbalance of power. In the case of an adult abuser and a child, the adult is clearly bigger, stronger, more experienced in life, and holds greater power. Children naturally look up to adults to guide them and provide rules for them to live by. Children also naturally try hard to please the adults in their lives, and trust them to know more than the child knows. When the adult uses their knowledge and experience (and ability to manipulate and lie, like in sexual abuse) to abuse the child, this is an abuse of adult power.

Human children have longer childhoods than any other mammals. All young mammals are vulnerable to predators: like the baby bunny who is vulnerable to the hawk from above.

But baby animals grow fast into smart adult animals and learn how to avoid predators. Because human children have longer childhoods, they are vulnerable for a longer period of time.

That vulnerability is what also makes abuse wrong. A child has less capacity, knowledge, and skill to protect themselves from predators. The predator takes unfair advantage of the child.

Some abusers were abused themselves as children, and say things like: "I got the strap when I was a kid, so I'm going to do the same to my kid." Or, "That's what happened to me as a kid, and I turned out OK, so it's OK to do it to my kid." Or, "If you would behave, this wouldn't happen." Or, "I was just teaching him/her what they need to know about sex." All of these statements are wrong.

Each child who is abused in some way reacts to the abuse a bit differently. Some children grow up and have only a few issues about their abuse, while other children grow up and have many issues that affect their adult lives due to the abuse. It does not matter how many or severe the issues are due to the abuse, it's still wrong and a crime.

Some Questions to Think About:

Did your abuser tell you that the abuse was your fault, or you somehow "made" the abuser abuse you?

Did you have a sense that what your abuser was saying and doing was wrong?

If you did not think it was wrong at the time, how old were you when you discovered that it was wrong?

If you did not think it was wrong at the time, do you now feel guilty or bad that you did not know it was wrong?

What is PTSD ?

"Post Traumatic Stress Disorder" is a way of describing the aftereffects of something very frightening. Child abuse is often very frightening to a child. The fear and abuse can damage how a child interacts with others, including family, friends and teachers. These effects can continue even after the abuse has stopped. The effects can follow a person into their adult life.

PTSD can cause many symptoms in a person. These symptoms come from the changes in your body and brain chemistry that happens when you are extremely frightened (like in child abuse). Your brain makes chemicals when you are very frightened or stressed. These chemicals then tell your body to either fight or run away from the abuse. In some cases, the person may just shut down when they are being abused, and let their mind "go somewhere else." You may become very upset, or frightened, angry, or anxious very easily. This can happen when something reminds you of your abuse. Other symptoms might be that your emotions feel "numb." You may be frightened to get close to people because of the abuse, and may avoid places or people that remind you of the abuse. It may feel at times as if the abuse is happening all over again, because the memories are so intense.

Survivors of child abuse with PTSD may find it difficult to have calm and satisfying relationships. The person might see the world as a very dangerous place, or a place where they always need to be looking around for danger, or are waiting for bad things to happen.

Many of these symptoms happen very fast. A person may be feeling fine and happy one moment, and then get very angry or agitated the next moment. They may feel like they want to fight the person who is near them, or that they want to run away, but don't know why or where they should go. Many people with PTSD feel like they are different from other people, or even that they are "going crazy."

The good news is that these symptoms can go away with hard work. Your brain and body learned these reactions at the time of the abuse as a way to cope with it. So, your body and brain can unlearn these reactions. You need to make the symptoms go away or at least ease up, because they make your life difficult and you do not need them anymore.

This workbook is all about just how to make the symptoms ease up and even go away. Your bad memories will always be with you, and those traumatic events will always be part of who you are. But you do not have to live with the terrible feelings and symptoms that are likely bothering you every day.

Some Questions to Think About:

Do you recognize any of the symptoms listed?

Why do you think that the bad memories and symptoms that happened when you were a child are still affecting your life now?

What does the article say about brain chemistry and PTSD symptoms? Did this surprise you?

Do people around you tell you about your symptoms?

What does the article say is the solution to making the symptoms stop?

PTSD Symptoms

One of the physical symptoms of PTSD is *agitation*. When a person with PTSD is "cued," they may "trigger" into a PTSD episode. A "cue" is something either in the world around you, or a memory, that reminds you of the abuse. This can then "trigger" your brain to make the chemicals that tell you to fight or run away. The same thing happened during your abuse.

When this happens, it is very uncomfortable. The brain chemicals make your *heart go faster*, you begin to *breathe faster*, and your *blood pressure rises*. Your *muscles might become tense*, and you may have an urge to *get up and walk around*, or even *to get away* from the place you are at. Some people might feel *lightheaded* or find it difficult to pay *attention* during a stress episode. Many people have *strong emotions* during this time, ranging from a general *uneasiness* to intense *fear* to strong and *explosive anger*. The uncomfortable feeling might last just a few moments, or hours or even days.

Some people who have been abused as children may have *aches and pains* that they cannot explain. They may feel *nauseous* or feel like they have to *go to the bathroom* a lot. They might have *"phantom pain."* This means a part of their body that was injured during their abuse as a child might begin to hurt or ache. For people who were sexually abused as children, they may have *pain during sex* when they are adults. Or, they may have problems being comfortable and *experiencing pleasure* during sex.

Some other people may feel emotionally or physically *"numb'* or feel like they are *in a "daze"* at times. They may have *bad memories* that just pop up during the day. The trauma may have changed how they see the world and themselves.

People who were abused as children often have problems with *sleep*. They might have a hard time going to sleep, or staying asleep, or getting enough deep sleep that refreshes them. They may have *nightmares* that are very disturbing. The nightmares may or may not be about the actual abuse that they suffered.

Some survivors find that when they feel stressed, they turn to *overeating* or *abusing substances* like alcohol or illegal drugs to help make the stressed feelings ease or go away. This can lead to *addiction* to these things, which complicates their lives even further.

For the purposes of the Stress Profile quiz later in the workbook, major symptoms of PTSD fall into these categories: physical and emotional agitation, re-experiencing, avoidance, numbing and detachment, relationship problems, psychological alterations, and changes to self structure.

Some Questions to Think About:

Do you have any of the symptoms listed in the article? Which ones?

How long have you experienced these symptoms?   weeks   months   years

When you have the symptoms, how long do they last?   seconds   minutes   hours   days

Can you feel when you body begins to react to a cue? What does this feel like to you?

Anxiety

Anxiety is a symptom (something that you experience) that can be very uncomfortable. One way to recognizing anxiety is by thinking of it as "worry," but anxiety is more than just worrying about something. Sometimes, a person is not really worried about anything in particular, but has all of the symptoms of anxiety.

The things that people feel when they are anxious can vary from having an upset stomach to headaches, aches and pains, or feelings like they have to run away or get out of a certain place. They may also sometimes feel like they are being watched or are in danger, and they can begin to feel like they have to be ready for a fight. It can feel like it is hard to breathe, or that you are going to pass out. Some people find it hard to stop thinking about a certain problem or chore that they have to do, or if someone in their life is going to do (or not do) something. All of these things can make focusing on the things you have to do quite hard.

Many people have a lot of anxiety and do not even know that they have it. That is because they have lived with anxiety for so long, they are kind of used to it. Their anxious feelings might come and go in intensity, but they always have it. Learning about your anxiety and how to cope with it and manage it is a very helpful thing to do.

Some Questions to Think About:

Do you get anxious or worry a lot?

What about?

How do you know when you are anxious?

Does your anxiety give you physical symptoms or thinking symptoms?

Hyper-Vigilance

One of the symptoms that abuse survivors often feel is hyper-vigilance. This is something that you feel, and may cause you to behave in ways that others find strange. The sensation of being hyper- vigilant is uncomfortable, like something bad is about to happen, or you have to "keep watch" so that nothing bad does happen.

Depending on the type of abuse you suffered, hyper-vigilance can include some of the following emotions and behaviors:

- Being edgy.
- Being worried.
- A nervous feeling.
- Feeling like someone is watching you.
- Feeling like something bad is about to happen.
- Feeling like you do not know what to expect from other people, especially the abuser.
- Needing to check over your shoulder or behind you frequently.
- Needing to check that doors or windows are locked.
- Needing to know where the people you care about are at all the time.
- Feeling very uncomfortable with certain behaviors, like hugging, touching, or sex.
- Being startled very easily.
- Having a difficult time sleeping; "keeping one eye open."

Some Questions to Think About:

Do you experience any of the symptoms of hyper-vigilance?

When do you have those feelings the most?

How long does the feeling last?

Do you have a way to make the feeling go away?

Memory Impairment

At the time you experienced your traumatic event, your brain went into overdrive, trying to help you to survive the event. Because it was so busy, your brain may not have been paying too close attention to the details about the event. Survivors often find that they have gaps, or "missing time" in their memory of the trauma. This can be disturbing to the survivor, because normally, their memory for things in every day life is quite good.

A survivor's memories of the event might come back in bits and pieces over time. How much time? It could be weeks, months, or even a lifetime. Some parts of the trauma may never be remembered by the survivor. Though this feeling is uncomfortable, it is a perfectly *normal* thing to happen during such an *abnormal* event!

Some survivors find that when they are cued and triggered by something that reminds them of their trauma, the resulting stress episode, and their behaviors during the stress episode are also difficult to remember. This too is expected, but it is important to understand that even if a survivor cannot clearly remember the things they or others did during a stress episode, the survivor is still responsible for their own behaviors. It is not acceptable to use PTSD as an excuse for poor behaviors.

Some Questions to Think About:

Do you think this is something that happens to you?

Have you found that there are things missing from your memory about the abuse?

Have you found that there are things missing from your memory about your childhood?

Have you gotten more memories as you have gotten older?

Depression

All of the bad feelings that can happen after a person has survived abuse and trauma can begin to kind of "mix together" and this can end up making a survivor feel very sad and depressed. If your trauma was ongoing, it may have felt like it would never end, and that can be very depressing. Most child victims of abuse come to understand at some point that not every child in the world has been abused and traumatized. They may suddenly realize that they feel different from other children. This is a very isolating, lonely and sad feeling.

Other feelings that abuse related depression can produce are: irritability, difficulty sleeping, feeling hopeless and helpless, loss of appetite, trouble sleeping or sleeping too much, not really enjoying things that used to be fun, and thoughts of self harm.

Some Questions to Think About:

Do you have any of the signs of depression listed?

Are you depressed right now?

Do you get depressed when you think of the past?

Did you feel different from other kids?

Do you feel different from other people your age?

Anger and Rage

A person who has been abused is often very angry at the person who hurt them, did not take care of them, or frightened them. When someone bigger than you does things to you that you don't want, or hurts you and you cannot fight them off or run away, or hide from them, anger and rage are only natural. This is because children, just like adults, need to have the feeling that they have some control over the things that happen to them. They also want to feel safe and secure, and get angry when the adult who hurt them takes that feeling away by their actions.

Simple anger may not be a strong enough word for what some survivors feel. Some get strong feelings of *rage* that are very powerful and frightening to themselves and other people around them. When a survivor feels rage, it may feel as if they are barely in control, or might do something really harmful to someone or themselves. Some people become verbally aggressive or physically aggressive, destroy property, or engage in risky behaviors when they experience anger and rage related to their abuse. However, this does not need to happen, and you can learn how to avoid harmful things when you experience it.

Some Questions to Think About:

Can you find your anger about your abuse?

What makes you most angry about your abuse?

Is the word 'anger' too small, does the word 'rage' seem a better description?

How do you experience the anger and rage you feel about your abuse? What things do you do when you are angry?

Fear

If the trauma that happens with abuse could be summed up in one word, it might be "fear." Far more than just worry or even anxiety. Many survivors experienced intense fear at the time of their abuse. Sometimes, "fear" is not a strong enough word for what a child feels, and the word "*terror*" comes closer to the real experience. Other children may not experience intense fear at the actual time of their abuse (as in some cases of emotional or sexual abuse), but later feel intense fear when thinking about it or being reminded of it.

This intense fear can come back when a survivor is cued and triggered. This may happen in situations where there is nothing really to be frightened about, but the survivor cannot stop the feeling of being deeply afraid. There also may be times when the fear is not so intense, but is still there in the "background," at a low level for extended periods of time.

Some Questions to Think About:

Do you find that you become frightened easily?

Do you find that you become frightened when there is nothing to be frightened of?

What was the most frightening thing about your abuse?

Does the word 'fear' or 'terror' fit better for your abuse experience?

Chapter 3 – How Abuse Affects our View of Ourselves and the World

View of the World

Once a person has been abused, their view of how the world works and how safe the world is changes. And since many survivors have been abused by family members or friends of their family, they begin to feel as if there is no place in the world that is actually safe. Children learn to feel safe or feel unsafe from the adults in their lives. If those adults are engaging in unsafe behaviors, like abusing substances, doing illegal activities, or consistently abusing the child, the child will view the world as a very dangerous place.

Children naturally learn trust from the adult caregivers in their lives. If a child is abused by a caregiver (like a parent), the child grows up believing that people are not trustworthy and are dangerous. Children who cannot trust begin to have problems in school with their learning and socializing.

Some Questions to Think About:

Did the world seem scary to you when you were a child?

Did you have any adult who made you feel safe?

Who did you trust the most when you were a child?

Whom could you not trust when you were a child?

Do you think how you look at the world changed because of your abuse? How?

View of Self

When a child is abused by an older person, especially a family member, it can change how the child views themselves. Children need to know that they are loved. Most parents and family members show this love with kindness, care, and guidance. When a child is abused, they may begin to think that they are being hurt because there is something wrong with them, or they are not a good person, or they are not lovable. These feelings lead to poor self esteem, and this sets up the child to possible beginning to engage in some unhealthy behaviors.

When you have the experience that another person can invade your space, even your body, whenever they want to, and you are powerless to stop it, you may begin to think of yourself as being owned by the other person. When you do not feel like you have control over your own body, you may begin to "lose" your sense of self.

Some Questions to Think About:

Did you feel loved when you were a child?

Who did you feel love from?

Did you ever feel like you were "owned" by your abuser?

Did you feel that there was something wrong with you, that you deserved the abuse?

Did you have a good self esteem when you were a child?

How is your self esteem right now?

Losing It

Emotional and psychological symptoms for survivors can sometimes get very overwhelming. Once a survivor is cued and triggered, all of the emotions already mentioned may happen at once, and they feel like they are "losing it," or having a "meltdown." This means that the person begins to feel unable to regulate their own emotions, and they are out of control. In therapy terms, when this happens for a PTSD survivor, we call it a "stress episode."

Though it *feels* like you are out of control, you are *not* out of control. That out-of-control feeling comes from the time when your abuse happened and you really were not in control of the situation and resulting trauma. Feeling like you are losing it is a very intense feeling, but it *can* and *will* ease, if you make good effort to learn how to heal yourself. The way you begin to do this is to learn about how stress reactions work in your brain and body, and how you can learn to modulate the reactions.

Some Questions to Think About:

Do you have stress episodes the way they are described above?

Can you tell when a stress episode is starting?

Are you able to interrupt it when it begins?

Does it seem that sometimes you stress episodes are started by little things?

Do you have intense memories when you have a stress episode?

Urge to Self-Harm

All the rage and anger and frustration that a survivor feels needs to go somewhere. In most cases, when the survivor was a child, they could not safely express their anger and rage towards their perpetrator. If they did so, they may get more abuse of some sort. Some victims turn all that anger toward themselves and begin to self-harm. Or, the victim feels so "numb" that they begin to self-harm so that they can *feel* at least *something*.

Sometimes a child who has been abused begins to feel helpless and hopeless, along with feelings of being worthless. Some children even begin to feel like they are "bad" or "evil" because of what their perpetrator tells them. As a result, they may have strong urges to self-harm. This self-harm can range from "cutting" to engaging in risky activities, or outright dangerous behaviors. Some even get so desperate that they make suicidal gesture or attempts.

Some Questions to Think About:

Have you ever deliberately hurt yourself?

Do you self- harm now?

If so, how do you self-harm?

Who else knows about your self-harm?

Have you thought about or tried suicide?

If your answer is "yes," and you feel this way now, please call someone your trust or a mental health center right away!

Self-Defeating Behaviors

Many survivors have had their self esteem damaged by their abuse. When your self-esteem is damaged and low, you may engage in what is called "self-defeating behaviors." This means that because you do not have healthy self-esteem, you place yourself in situations that are bad to be in. This may include being attracted to people who mistreat you or further abuse you. It also may mean that you abuse alcohol or drugs, or you miss a lot of work, school, or important appointments.

People who do these things and have a history of being abused as children are often told by others that they are "wasting their potential" or "you are better than that," or "you need to hang around a better class of people." You may recognize that you have a pattern of certain types of behaviors, like setting yourself up for failure by starting a very good thing, then messing it up in some way.

Stopping self-defeating behaviors can be difficult, but not impossible. The key to ending this self-sabotage lies in learning as much as you can about how abuse works in relationships, and how abuse as a child can affect your other relationships in life.

Some Questions to Think About:

What self-defeating behaviors do you have?

Can you see a pattern in your self-defeating behaviors?

Do you ever seem to "set yourself up for failure?"

Codependency

One important set of self defeating behaviors to become aware of is "codependency."

People who are survivors of child abuse may have had a number of years of the abuse. When this happens, a child has learned a very unhealthy way of being in relationship. In fact, some survivors get into an interaction pattern with their abuser that becomes ingrained, and a very strong habit. So much so that they may enter adult relationships that end up being very similar to the one that they had with their abuser.

Why this happens at first seems to make little sense: why would you hook up with other people who will abuse you just like your childhood abuser did? Other than learning to be in relationship this way or doing it out of habit, one other theory is: victims try and work through their original abuse that happened as a child with their new relationships.

But the best way to work through those abuse issues is to go to work on understanding them and finding other, healthier ways of working through them...like doing the work in this workbook, or entering counseling with a qualified counselor.

Some Questions to Think About:

Do you think you are codependent on someone? Who?

Which theory of why you tend to be codependent do you think is true for you?

Have you considered entering counseling to help you work through your abuse issues?

If you are uncomfortable with counseling, do you know why?

Attachment and Intimacy Problems

When a person has been hurt in some way by someone, it can make it hard to become attached to others and feel intimacy with them. Another way of saying attachment or intimacy is "feeling close." Some people with PTSD have a hard time feeling close to others in their life.

If, for example, when you were young, one of your parents sometimes took care of you well and sometimes did not take care of you properly, you may develop problems with attaching to others. This happens because a child can get very confused when a parent is kind and nice one moment, but mean and ignoring the next.

If a child is physically abused by a family member, this damages the child's sense of love and care in the family. Feelings of rage and anger toward the abuser keep healthy attachment to others difficult to do.

Some Questions to Think About:

Do you have hard time getting close to people?

What does it feel like when you get too close to a person?

Who did you feel most close to when you were a child?

Who do you feel most close to now?

Trust Problems

Once a person you have trusted betrays you and abuses you in some way, it becomes hard to not only trust that person, but other people too. It only stands to reason that we place *more* trust in people we know and people who are supposed to be caring for us than strangers. If your abuse happened more than once, and you were unable to predict when it would happen, this further damages trust in people. You feel that you have to be on guard at all times, not just around your perpetrator, but around other people that you know even less well.

When people have problems with trust, it can negatively affect their relationships with partners, children, friends, and other family members. It can produce a very lonely feeling.

Some Questions to Think About:

Is it hard for you to trust people?

Who did you trust most as a child?

Who did you want to trust, but could not?

Who do you trust most now?

What does a person have to do to earn your trust?

Broken Relationships

People who have been abused by those close to them often find that they have trouble in making and keeping relationships. This might be because at the first real or imagined sign of trouble in a relationship, you might end the relationship instead of taking the risk that it too will become abusive. Or, many people choose not to tell or tell very little about their abuse to others, even those that they are in a romantic relationship with. If you have not worked out your abuse and come to terms with it, you might find that the abuse starts to negatively impact the relationship.

Some Questions to Think About:

Do you have a history of broken relationships with people? Who?

Is it hard for you to make and keep friends?

Is it hard for you to stay in a love relationship?

Have you kept your abuse history secret?

Make a list of your broken relationships.

Chapter 4 – Understanding the Effects of Abuse

Effects of Childhood Neglect

If, as child, you have experienced shortages and have been deprived of needed things like food, medicine, the proper clothing, or the care and attention of an adult, you may have feelings of neediness that follow you into adulthood. It may seem as if you are constantly worried about "having enough" food, clothes, attention, or other things. You might argue with those around you about such things as saving money, or how money is spent, or get upset when you see wastefulness. Other people might describe you as stingy at times, and not wanting to share. You may find that you expect a great deal from those that you love, like a romantic partner. Your partner may tell you at times that you are "too smothering" and that they "need space" from you. On the other hand, you may find that you get accused of ignoring or not-paying enough attention to those close to you.

Some Questions to Think About:

Do you have any of the symptoms listed above?

Did you ever think that the cause of the symptom was your abuse?

What was the worst part of your experiences of neglect?

Are you demanding and have high expectations of those around you?

Effects of Childhood Physical Abuse

If you were physically abused as a child, you may have developed a "victim mentality." This is when a person who was physically abused as a child goes on to love relationships where their partner physically abuses them. Some victims move from one abusive partner to another, over and over. Even if your partner is not physically abusing you, you may be in a relationship of emotional abuse. On the other hand, you may have a hard time keeping relationships going past a certain point, because you get fearful that if your partner gets too close, they may start to hurt you. Or, you may worry that and you may begin to hurt them in the way you were hurt as a child.

Some Questions to Think About:

Did you feel like a victim at the time of your physical abuse?

Do you still feel like a victim?

Did you have a pattern of relationships where people physically abuse you?

Do you find that you reach a point in a relationship when you begin to feel anxious about the person beginning to abuse you?

Effects of Childhood Emotional Abuse

If you experienced emotional abuse as a child, you may struggle with your self-esteem. For many, this can lead to a string of failed relationships with partners who continue the emotional abuse pattern. You may feel "trapped" in your current relationship because emotional abusers use many psychological tricks to make the victim believe that they cannot survive without the abuser. As a result, you may stay with your partner because you think and feel that no one else in the world would ever want to be with you.

Some Questions to Think About:

How would you rate your self-esteem?

Do you think that your history of emotional abuse has anything to do with this?

Have you found that there is a pattern in your life of relationships with people who abuse your emotions?

Do you ever feel like other people are responsible for your feelings?

Effects of Sexual Abuse

Sexual abuse of a child can have devastating effects on a person's sexuality as they get older. If this has happened to you, you may have difficulty in finding a satisfying and relaxed sex life. Sexual activity, even with a partner you love and feel safe with, can cue and trigger memories and emotions for you that interrupt your sex life. There may be a particular sexual activity that is especially emotionally and psychologically (even physically) painful for you. You should remember that you should not do any sexual activity that you do not want to.

Some Questions to Think About:

Do you believe that your sexuality has been negatively affected by your history of sexual abuse?

If so, how has it been affected?

Are there particular sexual activities that cause you to have memories of the abuse?

If you have a current partner, have you told them about the history of your abuse?

From Victim to Survivor: a Change in How You See Yourself

An important step in recovering from child abuse is to change how you see yourself. At the time of your trauma, you were a victim of a crime. But you did what you needed to do to survive that terrible crime against you. Hopefully, you are no longer a victim of any current abuse. You have *survived* and come through your abuse, and you should be proud of that fact. Refuse to be a victim of abuse ever again! In order to become a survivor rather than a victim, you need to work at your own healing. If you are reading this and have done work in the workbook, then you are well on your way to being a survivor!

Some Questions to Think About:

Do you see yourself as a victim or a survivor of your abuse, or somewhere in between?

Does it sound odd to you to read: "Be proud that you're a *survivor* of abuse!"

What has your path been to move from a victim to a survivor? What things have helped you along the way?

Chapter 5 – Becoming a Successful Survivor

From Survivor to Thriver: Growth Beyond Survival

Your experience of child abuse does not have to continue to negatively affect your current life and relationships. You can move from being a survivor to taking hold of life and becoming a thriver. A person begins to thrive when they get to a certain level of healing, and they begin to shape their *own* life, their *own* way. This usually involves growing in many ways. It may mean that you enter into higher education, or develop a spiritual life, or you spend some time in counseling to rediscover who you are, aside from the trauma that you have survived. It means that you begin to be happy, satisfied, and serene.

Some Questions to Think About:

Being a Thriver means that you take charge of your own life and your own destiny. Do you feel that you have made this step yet?

If so, how did you do it?

If not, what do you see as the steps needed to get to Thriver?

Growth is key to thriving. What goals for further growth do you have?

Being Gentle With Yourself

People who have experienced interpersonal trauma often go through a period where they blame themselves for the abuse that happened to them. Even though one part of their brain says that this is ridiculous, there are strong thoughts that they are somehow to blame for what happened. Or, they feel that they should be punished for having "allowed" the abuse to take place. As a result, they may begin to actually punish themselves by engaging in self harm (like cutting), substance abuse, or promiscuity.

It is important to work at giving up the idea that you are to blame or that you could have stopped the abuse, or that you should punish yourself. It is important for you to learn to be gentle with yourself. Abusive behavior is the opposite of gentleness and nurturing. It's OK for you to nurture yourself and be gentle with yourself, or to invite someone you trust into your life to help you with nurturing and gentleness.

Some Questions to Think About:

Do you have a pattern of punishing yourself?

Did or do you blame yourself for the abuse?

What nurturing things do you do for yourself?

Learning to Feel Safe Again

Following abuse/trauma, people seldom feel very safe in their environment, or may only feel safe in certain places or with certain people. Learning to feel safe in most places and with most people takes time and effort. Feeling safe in places or around people who remind you of your trauma is especially difficult. Learning to feel safe includes getting some counseling to help you change how you think and behave regarding issues, people, and places associated with your trauma.

While you need to work at this, you should not push too hard to feel safe everywhere with everyone. Sometimes, it is wise to be cautious. Do the things that you need to do to feel safe, but be sure that these things are healthy things, not drinking or using drugs. Activities that might make you feel safe are things like making sure doors and windows are locked, always having your cell phone with you, having a dog with you, or even having a stuffed animal to hold when you feel unsafe.

Some Questions to Think About:

Do you feel safe most of the time?

Where and who with do you feel the safest?

Do you think your traumatic event(s) taught you to feel unsafe?

What do you do to help yourself feel safe?

Learning to BE Safe Again

A well-known effect of abuse that happens frequently is that the victim may develop what is called a *"victim mentality."* Due to the abuse, you may think of yourself as a victim, and as a person who does not deserve to be treated better. You may to enter into relationships where you are setting yourself up for continued abuse. A pattern may develop where each new relationship is just a repeat of the last one.

Learning to BE safe again first takes an understanding of the victim mentality and the details of how this works for an individual. For example, if you find that you are consistently attracted to a certain type of person, you may want to study why this is and make conscious changes about who you choose to be attracted to. It also means learning to read and pay attention to the "red flags" that are usually there in the relationship even at the beginning. For example, beating or neglecting a dog should be a big red flag about that person.

Some Questions to Think About:

Do you think you have or have had a "victim mentality?"

Have you set yourself up in bad relationships?

Can you recognize the "red flags" in your past?

Do you think it is possible to learn the details of your own "victim mentality?"

Learning Your Cues and Triggers

Learning about your own cues and triggers is an important area of work for recovery toward surviving and thriving. A good idea is to keep a "Cue and Trigger Journal." In the journal you can write down the cues and triggers you already know, and keep a brief description of any stress episodes you have. In reviewing the journal, you may discover other cues and triggers that you did not realize you had. For example, you might notice for the first time, due to journaling, that a certain time of day shows up in association with your cues and triggers.

Some Questions to Think About:

Do you know any of your cues and triggers?

What do you think about staring a "Cue and Trigger journal?"

Have you ever learned about a cue or trigger from someone else telling that they noticed that something cued or triggered you?

Learning to Recognize Your Reactivity Profile

Each person who has been through trauma and has PTSD is unique in experiencing the PTSD reactions. Some people have more intrusive memories or dreams, or have a strong feeling of numbness, while others have more detached and avoidant feelings or physical agitation. It can be helpful to learn about your own behavioral sign and symptom profile so that you know where to focus your attention best on your journey to healing. One way to do that is to use the Adolescent-Adult Stress Profile Tool on the next page.

The Adolescent-Adult Stress Profile can help you to understand your unique "stress profile" as related to your trauma history. It helps you to focus your work into particular symptom areas, and taking the Profile every few months can become a measure of your progress. Keeping a list of the signs indicated as "intense" can help you to identify possible cues and triggers.

Over time, the scores in the "frequent and intense" range should drop to "not frequent, but intense," and some of the "not frequent but intense" items should drop to "does not appear."

Some Questions to Think About:

Are you at a place in your healing process that you would be willing to learn about your "stress reactivity profile?"

If so, answer the questions on the Adolescent-Adult Stress Profile and then share them with your counselor, if you have one.

Adolescent-Adult Stress Profile

Directions: On the items that have a choice "a" or "b," only rate the question that best fits you, <u>not both</u>.

Scoring for each item: one of the 3 choices from the grid below or "D" for *Does Not Appear*

Symptom is...	Not Frequent	Frequent
Not Intense		*FN*
Intense	*NI*	*FI*

Question: *Do You....?*	Score
1. Do you have repeated traumatic events and/or abuse in your history?	
2 a. Do you currently experience intense stressors?	
2 b. Do you tend to create your own stress elements? (Procrastinate on work you need to do, overly dramatic in peer relationships, self sabotage).	
3 a. Do you struggle to adapt to novel situations?	
3 b. Do you start and then want to drop out of multiple activities? (Projects, commitments to others).	
4. Do you have prolonged stress responses that last for several hours?	
5. Do you have an inadequate response to danger, threat, or injury?	
6. Do you tend to over-react to small events?	
7. Do you tend to under-react to large events?	
8. Do you startle easily?	
9. Do you sometimes suddenly feel hyperactive?	
10. Do you have a difficult time calming down when upset or excited?	
11 a. Do you become verbally aggressive with little provocation?	
11 b. Do you have consistent irritability?	
12 a. Do you feel like running away or hiding when you feel threatened?	
12 b. Have you attempted or actually run away from home (overnight)?	
13. Do people sometimes tell you that you act like you are in "another world?"	
14 a. Do people tell you that your facial expressions become flat when you are upset?	
14 b. Do people tell you that you have rapid personality changes?	
15. Do you "freeze" when threatened?	
16. Do you get upset and stressed prior to or after contact with people associated with your trauma?	

17 a. Do you sometimes eat very fast, or overeat to the point of feeling sick?	
17 b. Do you have episodes of bulimia or anorexia, or have a generally excessive or low appetite?	
18 a. Do you seem to feel watchful, vigilant, or overly cautious?	
18 b. Do you think about or talk about how others hate you or are plotting against you?	
19. Do you ever feel "zombie-like" when you are upset?	
20. Do you begin to feel like a child when you get upset?	
21. Do you have a hard time telling others what you are thinking or feeling when upset?	
22. Do you sometimes seem to be upset (agitated) one moment, and fine (calm) the next?	
23. Do you easily forget about the stress episode that you just went through?	
24. Do you seem to have a hard time recalling what upset you after a stress episode is over?	
25. Do you seem to be upset for hours or days at a time?	
26. Do you have a strong urge to go to sleep following a stress episode?	
27. Do you ever stay upset, agitated, and hyperactive for more than a whole day?	
28. Do you talk about your trauma memories at times that are out of context?	
29. Do you have strong emotion when relating these memories?	
30. Do you have traumatic memories and feel little or no emotion?	
31. Do you have any places, situations, or items that seem to trigger a stress reaction? (If yes, list.)	
32. Do you have old injuries that hurt, or mysterious aches and pains?	
33. Do you have nightmares?	
34. Do you remember the content of the nightmares? (If yes, please list content.)	
35 a. Do you have a history of problems surrounding sexual relationships?	
35 b. Do people tell you that you are sexually provocative toward others?	
36 a. Do you seem to become emotional with someone, and it seems as if it really has to do with someone else?	
36 b. Do you tend to be consistently reactive rather than responsive in most interactions?	
37. Do you ever seem to be daydreaming and become emotional?	
38 a. Do you seem to have very fragile emotions?	
38 b. Have you had a previous or current diagnosis of bipolar disorder, ADHD, or Oppositional Defiant Disorder?	
39. Does it ever seem as if you repeat the same kinds of problems with different people?	

40. Do you ever speak to people who are not there? (hallucination)	
41. Do you have any anniversary reactions? (Times of the year that remind you of your trauma. If so, list them.)	
42. Do you tend to flinch at simple touch?	
43 a. Do you have the urge to hide items, food, or yourself?	
43 b. Do you collect and hide certain items (like tobacco, intoxicants, pornography)?	
44. When highly stressed, do the names or memories of perpetrators come to mind?	
45. Do you actively or passively avoid talking about your trauma or people associated with it?	
46. Do you actively or passively avoid contact with people or places associated with the trauma?	
47. Do you have times where you refuse affection or comfort attempts?	
48. Is it hard sometimes to have empathy for others?	
49 a. Do you bully or victimize others?	
49 b. Have you had problems bullying or being bullied on social networking sites?	
50. Do you ever mistreat or harm animals?	
51 a. Do you enjoy playing with fire?	
51 b. Do you have a fascination with, collect, or play with weapons?	
52 a. Do you try to minimize or hide your gender?	
52 b. Do you sometimes exaggerate your gender? (Dress 'macho' or sexually provocative clothes/makeup).	
53. Do you sometimes ignore or not give adequate attention to your personal hygiene?	
54. Do you sometimes not change your clothes for days?	
55. Do you sometimes have problems remembering facts about your trauma?	
56 a. Do you mix up the fact sequence about current events?	
56 b. Do you have the urge to tell lies that do not seem to have a purpose?	
57 a. Do you sometimes accuse others of things that they could not possibly have done?	
57 b. Do you find yourself lying to self-protect, or to harm others?	
58. Do you ever accuse others of doing things that were done by people associated with the trauma?	
59. Do you often feel apathetic, uninterested, bored?	
60 a. Do you verbally express low self-esteem?	
60 b. Are you clearly working below your ability?	

61 a. Do you choose to socially isolate?	
61 b. Do you turn down clear opportunities from peers to socialize?	
62 a. Do you have trouble engaging in cooperative tasks?	
62 b. Do you have consistent peer conflicts, sometimes to physical altercation?	
63 a. Do you become oppositional and defensive when given even simple directives?	
63 b. Do you frequently use foul language and offensive put-downs to others?	
64 a. Do you think you set yourself up for rejection in relationships?	
64 b. Do you have a compulsive need for a romantic partner at all times with frequent dramatic "breakups?"	
65 a. Do you have frequent friend changes?	
65 b. Do you form friendships with peers who you then get into trouble with?	
66 a. Do you often approach total strangers and start relationships?	
67 b. Do you find yourself attracted to people who are significantly older or younger than yourself?	
67. Does it ever feel as if it is hard for you to "connect" with others?	
68. Do you seem to jump to conclusions or misinterpret what others say?	
69. Does it feel like people are always teasing or shunning you?	
70 a. Do you have the urge to damage or destroy particular items in a methodical and predictable way?	
70 b. Do you create or are attracted to drawings, paintings, or computer images that are "dark" and disturbing?	
71. Do you have the urge to misbehave or demonstrate an emotion just to get attention?	
72. Do you get into frequent arguments with family members or peers?	
73. Do you engage in "stubborn" behaviors?	
74 a. Do you have trouble getting or staying asleep?	
74 b. Do you intentionally stay awake late into the night?	
75 a. Do you have trouble assessing danger?	
75 b. Do you seek out people who have bad reputations?	
76 a. Do you have bouts of explosive anger and rage?	
76 b. Do you have a history of punching walls, kicking doors, breaking glass, etc.?	
77. Do you seem to have focus and attention problems?	
78 a. Do you have the urge masturbate publicly or excessively?	
78 b. Do you have a history of making unwanted or crude sexual advances to peers?	
79. Do you often complain about being tired?	

80 a. Do you regularly engage in risky activities or play?	
80 b. Have you had involvement with police or juvenile probation?	
81 a. Do you often have feelings of despair?	
81b. Do you choose to adopt styles of dress or culture that are considered radical?	
82 a. Do you view the world as an excessively dangerous place?	
82 b. Do you avoid or refuse to participate in age-normal activities? (social events, community events.)	
83. Do you generally mistrust others?	
84. Do you feel very cautious around other people? (male, female, peers?)	
85. Do you have many secrets?	
86. Are you generally a secretive person?	
87. Do you have problems comforting yourself when upset?	
88. Do you self-comfort in unusual ways for your age? (Rocking self, stuffed animal, suck thumb, etc.)	
89 a. Do you have annoying thoughts about sex?	
89 b. Have you been or are you now sexually promiscuous?	
90 a. Do you tend to question every directive or request, no matter how simple?	
90 b. Have you had school or work discipline problems due to oppositional behaviors towards teachers or supervisors?	
91. Do you ever feel anxious that you will be abandoned by people you love?	
92 a. Do you ever feel excessively physically clingy toward others?	
92 b. Have you had incidents of inappropriate physical closeness to others?	
93. Do you insist on knowing where significant others are located at all times?	
94. Do you ever feel that you are to blame for the trauma?	
95. Do you seem to "lose it" or "melt down" when upset?	
96. Do you ever have a sudden feeling of panic?	
97 a. Do you engage in any self-harm behaviors?	
97 b. Do you ever do cutting, eraser burns, self tattooing, self piercing, substance abuse, etc.?	
98 a. Do you ever find it hard to stop thinking about a particular person associated with the trauma, such as the perpetrator?	
98 b. Do you tend to become obsessed (to the point of harassment) with a romantic interest, or other person?	
99. Do frequently feel ashamed or guilty?	
101 a. Do you seem to be a frequent victim of other people's meanness?	
101 b. Do you have a history of being victimized more than once?	
102. Do you have behavioral or mood changes after seeing particular people?	

Scoring the adolescent-adult stress profile: Indicate the number of each "intense" type response in each grouping. Note that on items that have two alternatives (a) or (b), count only the <u>higher</u> of the two ratings (FI)

Date: _____

Range	Sub-scale	D	FN	NI	FI
Items 1-27	Allostatic process and load (27)				
Items 28-44	Re-experience (17)				
Items 45-60	Avoidance, numbing & detachment (16)				
Items 61-72	Personal relationships (12)				
Items 73-90	Psychological alterations (18)				
Items 91-102	Self structure (12)				
	Totals				

Date: _____

Range	Sub-scale	D	FN	NI	FI
Items 1-27	Allostatic process and load (27)				
Items 28-44	Re-experience (17)				
Items 45-60	Avoidance, numbing & detachment (16)				
Items 61-72	Personal relationships (12)				
Items 73-90	Psychological alterations (18)				
Items 91-102	Self structure (12)				
	Totals				

Date: _____

Range	Sub-scale	D	FN	NI	FI
Items 1-27	Allostatic process and load (27)				
Items 28-44	Re-experience (17)				
Items 45-60	Avoidance, numbing & detachment (16)				
Items 61-72	Personal relationships (12)				
Items 73-90	Psychological alterations (18)				
Items 91-102	Self structure (12)				
	Totals				

In the author's clinical experience, most untreated survivors will score about half of the items in the "intense" range. It is recommended that the profile be reviewed and updated every few months to track progress.

Learning to Interrupt Your Reactivity

We all need some kinds of reactions. When we see the soccer ball flying at our face, we put our head down to protect our face and pass the ball, all without even thinking about it. But not all reactivity is a good thing. Stress reactions when there is no danger can make our life miserable. Learning to respond (instead of react) to a stressor, or a cue or trigger is ideal. But what do you do when the reaction has already started? While it is very tough to do, it is not impossible to interrupt a reaction. With practice, you get better at it.

An important tool is to pay attention to what you are thinking about in the moment of reaction. Those negative thoughts are the engine driving the reaction. When you identify the negative thoughts, you can consciously replace them with either neutral or positive thoughts. For example, if the negative thought is: "This situation is just like the one when my abuse took place," you might then try to find all of the ways that the situation is *not* like the one when your abuse took place. You might also add thoughts that while similar, the situation you are in is safe, and not dangerous like your abuse situation.

When you change your thinking, it should begin to help you calm your emotions. As you feel just a little bit better, you can take up the question: Is there something that I can *do* right now to help myself feel better? This might include leaving the situation that is cuing and triggering you, or getting support from someone who understands your stress reactivity.

Some people find that it helps to use an item to remind them to think about their thinking when they are cued or triggered. A special piece of jewelry, like a ring or bracelet, or a particular coin in their pocket may help.

Some Questions to Think About:

Do you notice a flood of negative thoughts when you are cued or triggered? If you don't notice, can you try and pay attention to what you are thinking the next time?

What are some things that you might find helpful to *do* once you are cued?

Is there an item that you could keep with you to use a reminder to use the process outlined?

Self-Calming and Self-Soothing of Mind and Emotion

When a person enters a stress reaction, their brain is giving them signals of danger, even when there is no danger present. The reaction at one time made very good sense, but it does not make sense in every situation where the triggering takes place. Learning how to override the automatic brain-body activity that causes the uncomfortable stress reaction is no easy task, but with practice, you can gain some degree of ability to interrupt the stress reaction process before it locks in full force.

To do this, the first task is to begin paying attention to what you are thinking. In most cases, the strong emotion you feel is associated with a flood of negative thoughts, such as "I'm unsafe here," or "I have to get away from this place, right now!" or "Something bad is going to happen." Taking a look around and challenging these kinds of thoughts with the reality of the situation (that you are safe) can begin to help soothe yourself.

Some people find that positive self talk can be helpful in combating the negative thoughts and emotions of a stress reaction. Others find that if they focus on engaging in some kind of meditation, or controlled breathing, or intense focus on a sound or a mantra (repeated positive word), they can also positively create calming for their thoughts and emotions. Still others find intense activity, like participating in sports, or dance, or a hard work hobby provides the same calming effect.

Some Questions to Think About:

Can you identify some of your own common negative thoughts when you are having a stress reaction?

What kinds of positive self talk might help you to calm yourself in the initial stages of a stress reaction?

Do you have any method of meditation or focus that could help you to calm your thoughts and emotions during the initial stages of a stress reaction?

Finding Meaning in Your Experience

Your traumatic experiences were horrible things to have happened to you. You did not deserve them. Once events happen to us, they will always be part of our history and who we are. Coming to acceptance of the reality of the abuse may take a survivor many years of hard work. Finding the reasons why the traumas took place also takes time. You may have asked many times over, "Why me?" You need to find your own answer to these questions.

But there may be something that goes beyond acceptance: finding *meaning* in the traumas that have happened to you. This is not to say that that your abuse was a good thing, but that you may be able to find a personal meaning that goes beyond the actual horrible events. Some survivors, for example, find that they turn their experiences into energy to combat interpersonal abuse for others, or work at trying to end abuse, or raising public awareness for a particular type of abuse.

Some Questions to Think About:

How far do you think you are from coming to a point of acceptance about your traumatic events?

Does finding meaning in the things that have happened to you seem like an odd idea?

What possible meaning could there be to your traumas?

About the Author

I grew up during the strange and turbulent 1960s and 70s in Erie, Pennsylvania. Though we were not dirt poor, my childhood family experience did not include the privileges and extravagances that I saw in the wider world. My three sisters and I were wealthy in perhaps a more important way: we had two spiritual, gentle, and firm parents in our home that was filled with love and care for each other.

My education, life experience, and vocational sense have always straddled the precarious space between secular and spiritual worlds. Having one foot planted in both worlds has allowed me to be in a unique place to meld the technical aspects of therapy with spiritual sensibilities like gentleness and compassion. My life journey has both gifted and burdened me with extensive experience in secular human services and spiritual ministry to adults, families, teens, and children.

This book was written with a passion to relieve the immense pain of children who have not had the idyllic and gentle upbringing that I had. My spirituality compels that when I see pain, I seek to heal it. If others who have similar callings read my work, perhaps more children will be healed. If others who have not yet recognized a similar calling read it, perhaps it will awaken in them at least a new awareness of the need for greater attention to these inured children.

When I begin to feel the pain of the work a bit too sharply, I try hard to be gentle with myself, and turn to my garden, or my watercolors, or to the deep woods to refresh myself. Anne, the love of my life for over thirty years, and my two fine sons, Andy and Tyler, continue to support me in my many ventures.

Each completion of a vocational task conceives and births the next... my curiosity about how to help a sexually abused child to heal their sexuality while they are still a child has grown from a passing thought in the midst of writing *Gentling* to my current insistent calling to apply these principles to this largely ignored area of treatment.

Glossary

Acute Stress Disorder: diagnosis from the Diagnostic Statistics Manual. It is essentially the same symptom set as Post Traumatic Stress Disorder, but is noted shortly after a trauma and up to six months afterward. Once the signs and symptoms are present longer than six months, the diagnosis becomes PTSD.

ADHD: diagnosis from the Diagnostic Statistics Manual. It stand for "Attention Deficit Hyperactivity Disorder".

Allostasis: essentially the process of physiological and emotional stress in the brain and body.

Allostatic load: The amount of physiological and emotional stress that an individual is experiencing in any given moment.

Behavioral Specialist: A clinical service provider who approaches the client's issues from a behavioral perspective, with planned behavioral interventions to effect positive change.

Child and Youth Services: county or state level child protection agencies designated to protect children from abuse and secure safe environments for them to live.

Child Stress Profile (CSP): a one hundred two item treatment focus and outcomes measure tool for children, and adolescents designed by the author.

Compassion fatigue: the effect of emotional 'burn out' on people who work in close and consistent contact with people who are injured, in pain, or in treatment.

Confabulate / confabulation: to fill in gaps of memory by fabrication, intentionally or unintentionally.

Cues: external or internal stimulus that serves as a conscious or unconscious reminder of a trauma or critical incident. The intensity of the cue may or may not trigger a stress reaction.

Decompensation: the emotional and psychological process of 'breakdown' of functionality due to intense stress or a mental health crisis.

Differentiation: a term originally coined by the father of family therapy, Murray Bowen. Expanded by subsequent clinicians to mean the ability to self regulate negative thoughts and emotions while remaining positively engaged with another.

Dissociation: a self-preserving mental and emotional process whereby the individual remains physically present, but psychologically and emotionally distances themselves from the present reality.

Dysregulation: the effect of not being able to self control or moderate one's negative thoughts and emotions, resulting in extreme behaviors.

Ego strength / ego wrapping: the sense the individual has of self integrity; the internal resources to be able to self regulate emotions and behaviors.

Encopresis: usually a non-medical source of bowel/fecal holding that results in 'overflow' soiling accidents.

Enuresis: accidental (or on occasion intentional) urine accidents, either during sleep or while awake, or both.

Galvanic skin response (GSR) monitor: a biofeedback tool that measures the very small electrical changes in the human body in response to stress; the tool uses an audible tone that rises or falls to indicate stress level.

Gentling: A protocol of clinical response to an individual who is experiencing a stress reaction related to Post Traumatic Stress Disorder. Also a comprehensive approach to children with PTSD as a result of interpersonal trauma.

Intense Range (on the CSP): PTSD related behaviors that present in such a way that the flow of daily life is disrupted significantly. Intense range is designated either 'Not Frequent', meaning less than once weekly, or 'Frequent', meaning weekly or more often.

Mobile Therapist: A clinician that goes to a client's home or school to provide services.

Pastoral Counseling: A clinical degree designation and discipline that takes account of a client's spiritual or religious history and practice, as well as making use of spiritual tools to enhance the clinical process of healing.

PTSD: the Diagnostic Statistics Manual diagnosis for individuals who have specific behavioral signs and experienced symptom of Post Traumatic Stress Disorder.

Quick Teach Pages: hand out educational sheets for collateral professionals in a case.

Reactive Attachment Disorder (RAD): a Diagnostic Statistics Manual diagnosis describing the disrupted pattern of human to human attachment that began very early in an individual's life. It is characterized by a kind of 'push-pull' of intimacy and rejection.

Rule-out: mental health behaviors and symptoms may at times be muddy or unclear, creating a 'rule out' diagnosis. This means that more information and evidences are needed to make a firmer decision about a diagnosis.

Secondary traumatization: the effect of one individual (usually a child) who develops *PTSD* symptoms from witnessing abuse of another individual (but not having been physically abused themselves). For example, a child who witnesses domestic abuse of their mother.

Stress episode / stress reactivity: The physiological process and resulting experienced symptoms and expressed behaviors of PTSD.

Stress-disordered: individuals who have a diagnosis of PTSD or ASD, as well as those individuals who have serious difficulty in coping effectively with stress.

Therapeutic Support Staff: professionals in the mental health field who hold a Bachelor's degree and help to carry out the therapeutic behavior intervention plan with children; an assistant or aide.

Triggering: the physiological process, which happens at lightning speed, of a cue 'triggering' a stress episode.

Triggers: a trigger can be a powerful *cue*, or the final cue of multiple cues that initiates the cascade of brain and body chemicals that results in a stress episode.

Bibliography

Ainsworth, M. D. S., Blehar, M. C., Waters, E., & Wall, S. (1978). Patterns of attachment: A psychological study of the strange situation. Hillsdale, NJ: Earlbaum.

American Psychiatric Association (2000). (DSM-IV-TR) *Diagnostic and statistical manual of mental disorders, 4th edition, text revision*. Washington, DC: American Psychiatric Press, Inc.

American Psychological Association Committee on Professional Practice and Standards (1998). *Guidelines for psychological evaluations in child protection matters.*

Appellee v. Bolin, In the supreme court of Tennessee at Knoxville, No. 03S01-9508-CC-00096 (1996).

Beers, S. and DeBellis, M. (2002). Neuropsychological function in children with maltreatment related posttraumatic stress disorder. *American Journal of Psychiatry,* 159:483-486, March 2002.

Berenson, K. (2006). Childhood physical and emotional abuse by a parent: transference effects in adult personal relations. *Personality and Social Psychology Bulletin,* Vol. 32, No. 11, 1509-1522.

Berry, J., & Jobe, J. (2002). At the intersection of personality and adult development. *Journal of Research in Personality,* Vol. 36, Issue 4, 238-286.

Bowlby, J. (1982). Attachment and loss: Vol. 1. Attachment (2nd ed.). New York: Basic Books (Original work published 1969).

Briere, J. & Elliott, D. (2003). Prevalence and psychological sequelae of self-reported childhood physical and sexual abuse in a general population of men and women. *Child Abuse & Neglect,* 27, 1205-1222.

Briere, J., & Elliott, D. (1997). Psychological assessment of interpersonal victimization effects in adults and children. *Psychotherapy,* Volume 34, Winter 1997, number 4.

Briere, J. (2006). Dissociative symptoms and trauma exposure: specificity, affect dysregulation and posttraumatic stress. *Journal of Nervous and Mental Disease,* Vol. 194(2), 78-82.

Briere, J., & Spinazzola, J. (2005) Phenomenology and psychological assessment of complex posttraumatic stress states. *Journal of Traumatic Stress,* Vol. 18, No. 5, 401-412.

Broderick, P. & Blewitt, P. (2006). *The Lifespan: Human Development for Helping Professionals.* Pearson Merrill Prentice Hall, New Jersey.

Bryant, R.A. (2007). Early intervention for post-traumatic stress disorder. *Early Intervention in Psychiatry*, 2007; 1: 19-26.

Carlson, B., McNutt, L., & Coi, D. (2003). Child and adult abuse among women in primary health care. *Journal of Interpersonal Violence*, Vol. 18, No. 8, 924-941.

Caspi, A. (1998). *Personality across the life course*. W. Damon (Ed.) Handbook of Child Psychology (5th Ed.). Vol. 3 Social, Emotional, and Personality Development. (pp 311-388). New York: John Wiley and Sons.

Caspi, A., & Moffitt, T.E. (1993). When do individual differences matter? A paradoxical theory of personality coherence. *Psychological Inquiry*, Vol. 4, No. 4, 247-271.

Caspi, A. & Roberts, B.W. (2001). Personality development across the life course: the argument for change and continuity. *Psychological Inquiry*, Vol. 12, No. 2, 49-66.

Ceci, S.J., & Bruck, M. (1995). *Jeopardy in the courtroom: a scientific analysis of children's testimony*. Washington, DC: American Psychological Association.

Cohen, J., Deblinger, E., Mannarino, A., & Steer, R.A. (2004). A multisite, randomized controlled trial for children with sexual abuse-related PTSD symptoms. *Journal of the American Academy of Child and Adolescent Psychiatry*, 43(4):393-402.

Cox, B., MacPherson, P., Enns, M., and McWilliams, L. (2004). Neuroticism and self-criticism associated with posttraumatic stress disorder in a nationally representative sample. *Behavior Research and Therapy*. Vol. 42, Issue 1, 105-114.

Crouch, J.L., Smith, D.W., & Ezzell, C.E. (1999). Measuring reactions to sexual trauma among children: comparing the children's impact of traumatic events scale and the trauma symptom checklist for children. *Child Maltreatment*, 1999.

Daud, A., Klinteberg, B., and Rydelius, P. (2008). Trauma, PTSD and personality: the relationship between prolonged traumatization and personality impairments. *Scandinavian Journal of Caring Sciences*.

DeBellis, M. (1999). Developmental Traumatology: Neurological Development in Maltreated Children with PTSD. *Child Maltreatment*, September 1999, Vol. XVI, Issue 9.

Depue, R.., & Collins, P. (1999). Neurobiology of the structure of personality: dopamine, facilitation of incentive motivation, and extraversion. *Behavioral and Brain Sciences*, 22;491-569.

Depue, R. (1995). Neurobiological factors in personality and depression. *European Journal of Personality*, Vol. 9, Issue 5, 413-439.

Englehard, I., van den Hout, M., & Kindt, M. (2003). The relationship between neuroticism, pre-traumatic stress, and post-traumatic stress: a prospective study. *Personality and Individual Differences*. Vol. 35, Issue 2, 381-388.

Erickson, S. (1999). Somatization as an indicator of trauma adaptation in long-term pediatric cancer survivors. *Clinical Child Psychology and Psychiatry*, Vol. 4, No. 3, 415-426.

Fauerbach, J., Lawrence, J., Schmidt, C., Munster, A, and Costa, P. (2000) Personality predictors of injury related posttraumatic stress disorder. *Journal of Nervous & Mental Disease.* 188(8):510-517.

Fonagy, P. (1999). Male Perpetrators of Violence Against Women: An Attachment Theory Perspective. *Journal of Applied Psychoanalytic Studies,* Vol. 1, No. 1.

Ford, J., Racusin, R., Ellis, C., Daviss, W., Reiser, J., Fleischer, A., & Thomas, J. (2000). Child maltreatment, other trauma exposure, and posttraumatic symptomology among children with oppositional defiant disorder and attention deficit hyperactivity disorder. *Child Maltreatment,* Vol. 5, No. 3, 2005-217.

Foster, J., & MacQueen, G. 2008. Neurobiological factors linking personality traits and major depression. *Canadian Journal of Psychiatry*, 53(1):6-13.

Green, Bonnie L., Krupnick, Janice L., Chung, Joyce, Siddique, Juned, Krause, Elizabeth D., Revicki, Dennis, Frank, Lori, Miranda, Jeanne. (2006). Impact of PTSD Comorbidity on One-Year Outcomes in a Depression Trial. *Journal of Clinical Psychology*, Vol. 62(7), 815-835.

Heim, C., Newport, J., Bonsall, R., Miller, A., & Meneroff, C. (2001). Altered pituitary-adrenal axis responses to provocative challenge tests in adult survivor of child abuse. *American Journal of Psychiatry*, 158:575-581.

Heinrivh, M., Wagner, D., Schoch, W., Soravia, L., Hellhammer, D., and Ehlert, U. (2005). Predicting posttraumatic stress symptoms from pretraumatic stress risk factors: a 2-year prospective follow-up study in firefighters. *American Journal of Psychiatry*, 162:2276-2286.

Hishaw-Fuselier, S., Heller, S., Parton, V., Robinson, L., & Boris, N. (2004). Trauma and Attachment: the case for Disrupted Attachment Disorder. J.D. Osofsky (Ed.), *Young children and trauma: intervention and treatment.* (pp. 47-68). New York: The Guilford Press.

Hunt, N., & Gakenyi, M. (2005). Comparing refugee and nonrefugees: the Bosnian experience. *Journal of Anxiety Disorders.* Vol. 19, Issue 6, 717-723.

Jumper, S.A. (1995). A meta-analysis of the relationship of child sexual abuse to adult psychological adjustment. *Child Abuse & Neglect,* 19, 715-728.

Kagan, J. (2000). Temperament. In A. Kazdin (Ed.), *Encyclopedia of Psychology.* New York: Oxford University Press.

Kamalla, L., Bruck, M., Ceci, S.J., & Shuman, D.W. (2005). Disclosure of child sexual abuse: what does research tell us about the ways that children tell? *Psychology, Public Policy, and Law,* 2005, Vol. 11, No. 1, 194-226.

Kaplow, J.B., Dodge, K.A., Amaya-Jackson, L., & Saxe, G.N. (2005). Pathways to PTSD, part II: sexually abused children. *American Journal of Psychiatry,* 162:1305-1310.

Karen, R. (1998). *Becoming attached: First relationships and how they shape our capacity to love.* New York: Oxford University Press.

Kemph, John P., Voeller, Kytja K.S. (2008). Reactive Attachment Disorder in Adolescence, Adolescent Psychiatry.

Knezevic, G., Opacic, G., Savic, D., and Priebe, S. (2005). Do personality traits predict post-traumatic stress: A prospective study in civilians experiencing air attacks. *Psychological Medicine*, 35:659-663.

Koenen, K. C. (2006) Self-regulation as a central mechanism. Psychobiology of Posttraumatic Stress Disorder: A Decade of Progress. Vol. 1071: 255-266.

Lauterbach, D. (2001). Personality profiles of trauma survivors. *Traumatology*, Vol. 7, No. 1.

Lauterbach, D., & Vrana, S. (2001). The relationship among personality variables, exposure to traumatic events, and severity of posttraumatic stress symptoms. *Journal of Traumatic Stress*, Vol. 14, No. 1, 29-45.

Lecic-Tosevski, D., Gavrilovic, J., Knezevic, G., and Priebe, S. 2003. Personality factors and posttraumatic stress: associations in civilians one year after air attacks. *Journal of Personality Disorders*, Vol. 17, Issue 6, 537-549.

Lester, P., Wong, S., Hendren, R. (2003). The Neurobiological Effects of Trauma. *Adolescent Psychiatry*.

Lieberman, A.F., & Van Horn, P. (2004) Assessment and treatment of young children exposed to traumatic events. J.D. Osofsky (Ed.), *Young children and trauma: intervention and treatment.* (pp.111-138). New York: The Guilford Press.

Lombardo, T.W., & Gray, M.J. (2005). Beyond exposure for posttraumatic stress disorder (PTSD symptoms. *Behavior Modification,* Vol. 29, No. 1, 3-9.

Marshal, R.D., Spitzer, R., & Liebowitz, M.R. (1999). Review and critique of the new DSM-IV diagnosis of acute stress disorder. *Journal of Psychiatry*, 156:1677-1685.

May, J. (2005). Family attachment narrative therapy: healing the experience of early childhood maltreatment. *Journal of Marital and Family Therapy,* July 2005.

McAdams, D., Bauer, J., Sakaeda, A., Anyidoho, N, Machado, M., Magrino-Failla, K., White, K., and Pals, J. (2006). Continuity and change in the life story: a longitudinal study of autobiographical memories in emerging adulthood. *Journal of Personality*, Vol. 74, Issue 5, 1371-1400.

Mrockek, D.K., & Spiro, A. (2003). The Journals of Gerontology Series B: Psychological Sciences and Social Sciences, 58:P153-P165.

Muller, R., Sicoli, L., & Lemieux, K. (2000). Relationship between attachment style and post traumatic stress symptomology among adults who report the experience of childhood abuse. *Journal of Traumatic Stress*, Vo. 13, No. 2.

Nader, K. (2001) Treatment Methods for Childhood Trauma. In Wilson, J.P., Friedman, M.J., & Lindy, J.D. (Eds.) *Treating psychological trauma & PTSD* (pp.278-334). New York: The Guilford Press.

Neuman, D.A., Houskamp, B.M., Pollock, V.E., & Briere, J. (1996). The long term sequelae of childhood sexual abuse in women: a meta-analytic review. *Child Maltreatment,* 1,6-16.

Oquendo, M.A., Friend, J.M., Halberstam, B., Brodsky, E. et al. (2003). Association of Comorbid Posttraumatic Stress Disorder and Major Depression With Greater Risk for Suicidal Behavior. American Journal of Psychiatry 160:580-582, March 2003

Paris, J. (2005). Neurobiological dimensional models of personality: a review of the models of Cloninger, Depue, and Siever. *Journal of Personality Disorders*, Volume 19, Issue 2, 156-170.

People v. Stritzinger, 34 Cal. 3d 505, 668 P.2d 738, 194 Cal. Rptr. 431 (1983).

Perry, B., & Azad, I. (1999). Post-traumatic Stress Disorders in children and adolescents. *Current opinions in Pediatrics,* Volume 11, number 4: (August 1999).

Perry, B. (2001b). The neurodevelopmental impact of violence in childhood. In Schetky D & Benedek, E. (Eds.) *Textbook of child and adolescent forensic psychiatry.* Washington, D.C.: American Psychiatric Press, Inc. (221-238)

Perry, B. Neurobiological sequelae of childhood of childhood trauma: post traumatic stress disorders in children. In: *Catecholamine Function in Post Traumatic Stress Disorder: Emerging Concepts* (M. Murburg, Ed.) American Psychiatric Press, Washington, D.C., 253-276, 1994.

Perry, B., & Pollard, D. Altered brain development following global neglect in early childhood. *Society For Neuroscience: Proceedings from Annual Meeting*, New Orleans, 1997.

Perry, B.. Neurobiological sequelae of childhood trauma: post traumatic stress disorders in children. In: *Catecholamine Function in Post Traumatic Stress Disorder: Emerging Concepts* (M. Murburg, Ed.) American Psychiatric Press, Washington, DC, 253-276, 1994.

Perry, B. (1996). *Violence and childhood trauma: Understanding and responding to the effects of violence on young children.* Grund Foundation Publishers, Cleveland, Ohio. 1996, pp. 67-80.

Perry, B.. & Pollard, D. Altered brain development following global neglect in early childhood. *Society For Neuroscience: Proceedings from Annual Meeting*, New Orleans, 1997.

Psychological first aid: filed operations guide, 2nd edition. (July 2006). Retrieved June 1, 2007 from http://www.ncptsd.va.gov/ncmain/ncdocs/manuals/smallerPFA_2ndEditionwithappendices.pdf.

Regan, J. Johnson, C., & Alderson, A. (2002) *Expert testimony linking child sexual abuse with posttraumatic stress disorder.* April 2002.

Richeters, M.M. and Volkmar, F.R. (1994). Reactive Attachment Disorder of Early Childhood. J. *Am. Acad. Child Adolesc. Psychiatry,* 33, 3: 328-332.

Roberts, B.W., Mroczek, D. (2008). Personality trait change in adulthood. *Current Directions in Psychological Science*, Vol. 17, No. 1, 31-35(5).

Roberts, B.W., DelVecchio, W.F. (2000). The rank-order consistency of personality traits from childhood to old age: a quantitative review of longitudinal studies. *Psychological Bulletin*, Vol. 126, No. 1, 3-25.

Roberts, B.W., Wood, D., Smith, J.L. (2005). Evaluating five factor theory and social investment perspectives on personality trait development. *Journal of Research in Personality*, 39, 166-184.

Ruchkin, V., Schwab-Stone, M., Koposov, R. Vermeiren, R., and Steiner, H. (2002). Violence exposure, posttraumatic stress, and personality in juvenile delinquents. *Journal of the American Academy of Child & Adolescent Psychiatry*. 41(3):322-329.

Schnarch, David. (1991). *Constructing the sexual crucible: An integration of sexual and marital therapy*. Norton Professional Books.

Schuder, M.R., & Lyons-Ruth, K. (2004). "Hidden trauma" in infancy: Attachment, fearful arousal, and early dysfunction of the stress response system. In J.D. Osofsky (Ed.), *Young children and trauma: intervention and treatment*. (pp. 69-106). New York: The Guilford Press.

Schore, A. (2002). Dysregulation of the right brain: a fundamental mechanism of traumatic attachment and the psychopathogenesis of posttraumatic stress disorder. *Australian and New Zealand Journal of Psychiatry*, 36(1):9-30, February 2002.

Schore, Allan, (2001) The effects of early relational trauma on right brain development, affect regulation, & infant mental health. *Infant Mental Health Journal*, 22, 201-269.

Schuder, M, and Lyons-Ruth, K. (2001). Hidden Trauma in Infancy. In Wilson, J.P., Friedman, M.J., & Lindy, J.D. (Eds.) *Treating psychological trauma & PTSD* (pp.69-104). New York: The Guilford Press.

Schwedtfeger, K.L. & Goff, B.S.N. (2007). Intergenerational transmission of trauma: exploring mother-infant prenatal attachment. *Journal of Traumatic Stress*, 20, 39-51.

Starasburger, L.H., Gutheil, T.J., & Brodsky, A. (1997). On wearing two hats: role conflict in serving as both psychotherapist and expert witness. *American Journal of Psychiatry*, 154:4, April 1997.

Vander Kolk, B. (1998) Re-enactment, Revictimization, and Masochism. *Psychiatric Clinics of North America*, Vol. 12, No. 2, 389-411. June, 1998.

Van Voorhees, Elizabeth. (2004). The effects of child maltreatment on the hypothalamic-pituitary-adrenal axis. *Trauma, Violence, & Abuse*, Vol. 5, No. 4, 333-352.

Victims of Child Abuse Act of 1990, Article IV.

Volkman, M. K. (2007). *Children and traumatic incident reduction: Creative and cognitive approaches*. Ann Arbor, MI: Loving Healing Press.

Walters, J.T.R., Bisson, J.I., & Shepherd, J.P. (2006). Predicting post-traumatic stress disorder: validation of the trauma screening questionnaire in victims of assault. *Psychological Medicine*, 37, 143-150.

Walters S; Holmes L., Bauer, G; Vieth, V. (2003) *Finding Words: Half a Nation by 2010--Interviewing Children and Preparing for Court*. US Dept of Health and Human Services.

Warner, Megan B., Morey, Leslie C., Finch, John F., Gunderson, John G., Skodol, Andrew, Sanislow, Charles A., Shea, Tracie M., McGlashan, Thomas H., and Grilo, Carlos M. (2004). The longitudinal relationship of personality traits and disorders. *Journal of Abnormal Psychology*, 113:217-227.

Watters, T., Brineman, J., Wright, S. (2007). Between a rock and a hard place: why hearsay testimony may be a necessary evil in child sexual abuse cases. *Journal of Forensic Psychology Practice*,. Volume: 7, Issue: 1.

Weine, S.M., Becker, D.F., Vojvoda, D., Hodzic, E., Sawyer, M., Hyman, L., Laub, D., and McGlashan, T.H. (2005) Individual change after genocide in Bosnian survivors of "ethnic cleansing": assessing personality dysfunction. *Journal of Traumatic Stress*, Vol. 11, No. 1, 147-153.

Wilson, J.P. (2001) An overview of clinical considerations and principles in the treatment of PTSD. In Wilson, J.P., Friedman, M.J., & Lindy, J.D. (Eds.) *Treating psychological trauma & PTSD* (pp.59-93). New York: The Guilford Press.

Wexler, R., (1995). *Wounded innocents*. Buffalo: Prometheus Books.

Wrightsman, L.S. (2005). *Forensic Psychology*. USA: Wadsworth.

Wonderlich, S.A., Crosby, R.D., Mitchell, J.E., Thompson, K., Smyth, J.M., Redlin, J., and Jones-Paxton, M. (2001). Sexual trauma and personality: developmental vulnerability and additive effects. *Journal of Personality Disorders*, Vol. 15, Issue 15, 496-504.

Young, S.N., Moskowitz, D.S. (2005). Serotonin and affiliative behavior. *Behavioral and Brain Sciences*, 28:367-368.

Zald, D.H., & Depue, R.A. Serotonergic functioning correlates with positive and negative affect in psychiatrically healthy males. *Personality and Individual Differences*, Vol. 30, Issue 1, 71-86.

NOTES

Breakthrough Treatment Offers New Hope for Recovery

Revised and Expanded 2nd Edition with 3 new chapters on adolescents

Gentling represents a new paradigm in the therapeutic approach to children who have experienced physical, emotional, and sexual abuse and have acquired Post Traumatic Stress Disorder as a result. This text redefines PTSD in child abuse survivors by identifying child-specific behavioral signs commonly seen, and offers a means to individualize treatment and measure therapeutic outcomes through understanding each suffering child's unique symptom profile. The practical and easily understood Gentling approaches and techniques can be easily learned by clinicians, parents, foster parents, teachers and all other care givers of these children to effect real and lasting healing.

With this book, you will:

- Learn child-specific signs of PTSD in abused children
- Learn how to manage the often intense reactivity seen in stress episodes
- Gain the practical, gentle, and effective treatment tools that really help these children
- Use the Child Stress Profile (CSP) to guide treatment and measure outcomes
- Deploy handy 'Quick Teach Sheets' that can be copied and handed to foster parents, teachers, and social workers

Clinicians Acclaim for *Gentling*

"In this world where children are often disenfranchised in trauma care--and all too often treated with the same techniques as adults--Krill makes a compelling case for how to adapt proven post-trauma treatment to the world of a child."

--Michele Rosenthal, HealMyPTSD.com

ISBN 978-1-61599-106-8   List $23.95

What if we could resolve childhood trauma early, rather than late?

We are understanding more and more about how early traumatic experiences affect long-term mental and physical health:

• Physical impacts are stored in muscles and posture
• Threats of harm are stored as tension
• Overwhelming emotion is held inside
• Negative emotional patterns become habit
• Coping and defense mechanism become inflexible

What if we could resolve childhood trauma before years go by and these effects solidify in body and mind?

In a perfect world, we'd like to be able to shield children from hurt and harm. In the real world, children, even relatively fortunate ones, may experience accidents, injury, illness, and loss of loved ones. Children unfortunate enough to live in unsafe environments live through abuse, neglect, and threats to their well-being and even their life.

Children and Traumatic Incident Reduction: Creative and Cognitive Approaches

Edited by Marian K. Volkman, CTS, CMF

Experts Praise *Children and TIR*

"This book is a must for any therapist working with kids. Naturally, it focuses on the approach of Traumatic Incident Reduction, but there is a lot of excellent material that will be useful even to the therapist who has never before heard of TIR and may not be particularly interested in learning about it. The general approach is respectful of clients, based on a great deal of personal experience by contributors as well as on the now extensive research base supporting TIR, and fits the more general research evidence on what works".

—Robert Rich, PhD

"Much useful and thoroughly researched information is packed into this priceless volume in the TIR Application Series. This is a good book for parents to read because s/he may take away an understanding of the many different therapy strategies available to them and their children."

—Lisa Bullert, *Reader Views*

ISBN 978-1-932690-30-9   List $19.95
More information at www.TIRbook.com

REPAIR For Kids

Recognition
Entry
Process
Awareness
Insight
Rhythm

Enter a Six–Stage Program with your child to cross the Bridge of Recovery and make available a whole new world of hope:
- Uncover and acknowledge feelings by discovering emotion
- Build self-esteem and optimism with the "Magic Mirror"
- Discern healthy and unhealthy messages
- Learn self-soothing skills with "Dear Diary" letters to the inner-child
- Reveal inner states with picture drawing
- Break free from the confines of false shame
- Cultivate self-care skills and practices
- Learn about boundaries and bodies
- Return to the natural rhythm and flow of life

"*REPAIR for Kids* provides a comprehensive, honest and passionate approach for children recovering from sexual abuse. Children will benefit from this book, and be encouraged to continue on their recovery journey.

—Jill Osborne, Ed.S,
author of *Sam Feels Better Now*

"I wish I had had something like this a long time ago for my sad and shamed 'little girl' within. I can't think of anything I'd change. You have covered it all and with wonderful sensitivity, perfect timing and terrific repair exercises. I love the cartoons and the colorfulness of your book as well."
—Marcelle Taylor, MFT

ISBN 978-1-932690-57-6   List $34.95
More information at www.TheLamplighters.org

CPSIA information can be obtained
at www.ICGtesting.com
Printed in the USA
BVHW011257090719
552965BV00007B/75/P